The Christian's Great Salvation

Timothy Cross

Day One

Endorsement

Dr. Martyn Lloyd Jones once said, 'The Christian is not a good man. He is a vile wretch who has been saved by the grace of God.' My friend and co-labourer, Timothy Cross, does an excellent job in this book, clearly and concisely proclaiming such a blessed salvation. Whether you are on the outside looking in or on the inside looking out, I strongly recommend this publication for your study and attention.

Pastor Rick Owens, Alvarado, Texas, USA

First published in Great Britain in 2021 by
Day One, Ryelands Road, Leominster, HR6 8NZ
Email: sales@dayone.co.uk
Website: www.dayone.co.uk

The right of Timothy Cross to be identified as the author of this work has been asserted by him in accordance with the Copyright, Designs and Patents Act 1988.

British Library Cataloguing in Publication Data available

ISBN: 978-1-84625-701-8

Cover design by Kathryn Chedgzoy

Printed by 4edge

To my brothers and sisters in Christ
at Cornwall Street Baptist Church,
Grangetown, Cardiff,
with grateful thanks for your priceless
fellowship and encouragement.

Contents

Introduction

In Revelation 7:10, we read of the exuberant praise uttered by the redeemed in glory. Their cry is: '*Salvation* belongs to our God who sits upon the throne, and to the Lamb!'

Salvation is the overarching theme of the Bible, the jewel in the crown of the Christian faith, and the cause of praise and wonder in every Christian who has come to know its joy. If we wanted to summarise the message of the Bible, we could say that its main message is God's salvation of His people through His promised Messiah, the Lord Jesus Christ—the Lamb who was slain to procure the salvation of God's people. The gospel of Christ is '... the power of God for *salvation* to every one who has faith' (Romans 1:16). The gospel of Christ is '... the word of truth, the gospel of your *salvation*' (Ephesians 1:13).

But what do we mean by salvation? Salvation refers to a deliverance or rescue from danger or peril. Biblically, salvation refers to *divine* salvation—God Himself to the rescue. According to the Bible, all three members of the divine trinity have a part in the believer's salvation; for a Christian is described as being 'chosen and destined by God the Father and sanctified by the Spirit for obedience to Jesus Christ and for sprinkling with His blood' (1 Peter 1:2).

Yet salvation refers to far more than a rescue from

danger—wonderful though that alone is. Salvation refers to the blessing of God Himself. Truth be told, salvation is the greatest blessing which we can or will ever receive. It is a blessing which this world can neither give nor take away, and it is a blessing which transcends this passing world. It has past, present and future facets to it. It refers ultimately to the highest joy—to being in fellowship with God our Maker for time and eternity.

Salvation is an all-embracing word and, in the following pages, we will explore some of the facets of the many-sided diamond which is Christian salvation—the salvation which God, through Christ, freely bestows on the believer in His amazing grace. Under the blessing of God, may this book prove useful in confirming Christians in their most precious faith, and even cause some to know and rejoice for the first time in the salvation which Christ alone can bring.

May God bless you as you read and weigh what follows. Ultimately, salvation is the most crucial matter of all. Hence the Bible's warning: 'How shall we escape if we neglect such a great salvation?' (Hebrews 2:3).

Timothy Cross
Cardiff
South Wales

Divine
redemption

'In Him we have redemption through His blood, the forgiveness of our trespasses, according to the riches of His grace.

Ephesians 1:7

Christian salvation concerns the matter of a great redemption—a redemption divinely accomplished and divinely applied. Redemption is a thread and theme which runs through the whole Bible. In Old Testament times, God *redeemed* His people—He freed them from cruel slavery in Egypt. This was a foreshadowing of a greater Redemption—the eternal redemption, which was accomplished by Christ for the believer when He shed His precious blood on Calvary's cross. Redemption is central to the Bible and central to the message of the Christian gospel. The gospel proclaims the good news of redemption, and invites, encourages and exhorts sinners to avail themselves of it. Redemption is accordingly the theme of a thousand Christian hymns, because Christians have a redemption to share, celebrate and sing about:

Redemption! Oh wonderful story
Glad message for you and for me
That Jesus has purchased our pardon
And paid all the debt on the tree

Believe it, O sinner, believe it
Receive the glad message – 'tis true

Trust now in the crucified Saviour
Salvation He offers to you.

Samuel M. Sayford (1846–1921)

Definitions

But what exactly do we mean when we speak of *redemption?*

To redeem means to purchase—to buy back by the expenditure of some effort or price. It also means to reclaim and means to free or to liberate. Slavery was part of the social fabric in Bible times. The Ephesians, to whom our opening verse was written, were well acquainted with the practice of slavery. Some may even have been slaves themselves. But a slave could be set free. A kindly benefactor with money could purchase the slave's freedom by paying a price to the slave's master. *To redeem* therefore means *to purchase and set free by paying a price.* But this implies a redeemer.

A redeemer is the one who accomplishes the redemption—the one who undertakes the recovery and redeeming work by paying the necessary price. Suffering Job in ancient times longed to be released from his plight, and cried out in faith, 'For I know that my Redeemer lives, and at last He will stand upon the earth' (Job 19:25). Job's longing was fulfilled in the fullness of time by the central figure of the Bible, the Lord Jesus Christ. The inspired Word points us to the Living Word. The Bible reveals that

Jesus' main office is that of Redeemer. It was to accomplish the sinner's redemption that Christ left heaven for earth:

> The only Redeemer of God's elect is the Lord Jesus Christ who, being the eternal Son of God became man and so was and continueth to be, God and man in two distinct natures and one person for ever (*Shorter Catechism*).[1]

Redemption itself then refers to a state of blessedness. It is the resultant state of freedom and happiness experienced both now and in the future by the recipients of the redeeming work of Christ the Redeemer, who did everything necessary to accomplish our redemption. Christians consequently are a liberated people. They have been set free from the guilt of sin and the penalty which they deserve for their sins because the Lord Jesus Christ has redeemed them. He purchased their salvation when He died on Calvary's cross. Jesus could therefore say 'If the Son makes you free, you will be free indeed' (John 8:36). The good news of redemption, however, is prefaced by some bad news.

Bad News

The good news of redemption makes no sense at all unless it is viewed and understood against the bad news of sin— that we are in dire and desperate need of redemption. Hence, we have a dire and desperate need for a Redeemer. The Bible teaches that we are sinners by nature and practice. We have all broken God's holy law as 'Sin is any want of conformity unto or transgression of the Law of God' (*Shorter Catechism*).[2]

Even in this life, misdemeanours render us liable to pay a penalty. If you park where you shouldn't, you will get a parking ticket telling you that you have to pay a fine, and this fine will increase the longer you delay in paying it. More serious offences may land you in jail. Breaking the law of the land, then, incurs a penalty. But breaking the law of God incurs an eternal penalty, known in the Bible as '… the curse of the law' (Galatians 3:13). Sin is serious because it is against Almighty God Himself and we are all guilty here, even if we are respectable in the eyes of the world. James 2:10 reminds us: 'For whoever keeps the whole law but fails in one point has become guilty of all of it.' Sin has to be paid for and sin will be paid for—either by the sinner in hell, or in the person of a substitute, if such a substitute could be found.

The Good News

The Christian gospel proclaims that on Calvary's cross Jesus paid the penalty for our sins when He became the sinner's substitute, so that all who believe in Him will be released from that penalty. 1 Peter 2:24 says, 'He Himself bore our sins in His body on the tree.' That means Christ Himself was made liable for our sins, so that when we believe in Him, we are released from that liability. The gospel proclaims that God's Own Son Paid Every Liability. Poetically:

> There was no other good enough
> To pay the price of sin
> He only could unlock the gate
> Of heaven and let us in.

Cecil Frances Alexander (1818–95)

The Christian faith is distinguished by a redemption which was accomplished by the Lord Jesus Christ. Other faiths all have in common the obligation for us to redeem ourselves by what we do. The Christian's redemption, however, rests and depends wholly and solely on Christ— His sinless life and atoning death. Do we then have to do anything to gain our redemption from sin? The answer is both no and yes. No, we don't need to do anything because Jesus has done it all by paying the penalty for our sins in full. But yes, we have to avail ourselves of Christ's redeeming work or else it will not profit us at all. How then do we avail ourselves of Christ's redeeming work and make all the blessings and benefits of redemption our own? The answer is this: *only through the mighty assistance of the Holy Spirit of God.* This takes us back to what we said at the outset, namely that Christian salvation is a matter of a redemption divinely accomplished and divinely applied. Specifically, it was accomplished by the Son of God, and it is applied to the human soul by the Spirit of God. The *Shorter Catechism* states:

How are we made partakers of the redemption purchased by Christ?

We are made partakers of the redemption purchased by Christ by the effectual application of it to us by His Holy Spirit.

How doth the Spirit apply to us the redemption purchased by Christ?

The Spirit applieth to us the redemption purchased by Christ, by working faith in us, and thereby uniting us to Christ in our effectual calling.[3]

In a nutshell, we can say that while Christ has purchased the sinner's redemption, it is the Holy Spirit who puts the sinner in actual possession of the redemption Christ purchased. How does He do this? He convinces us of both our need for Christ and the Christ for our need. He convicts us of our sin and liability—the curse for breaking God's law—and He reveals to us God's gracious provision for this deep, desperate and damnable need: the provision of the crucified Christ. 'Christ redeemed us from the curse of the law, having become a curse for us—for it is written, "Cursed be every one who hangs on a tree"' (Galatians 3:13). The Holy Spirit draws us to Christ, nurtures in us saving faith in Him, and enables us to receive all the benefits of Christ's redeeming work for ourselves. We put our trust in Christ and the joy of redemption floods our souls. We are saved by Christ, through the instrumentality of faith and the gracious working of the Holy Spirit in our hearts.

A Christian cannot claim to be perfect. Non-Christians can take great delight in pointing out our faults. But the united testimony of every Christian is, 'I am redeemed.' God's eternal promise for all who belong to Jesus is this: 'Fear not, for I have redeemed you; I have called you by name, you are mine' (Isaiah 43:1). Redemption is a Christian basic. So, we end our opening chapter as we began, and affirm, 'In Him we have redemption through His blood, the forgiveness of our trespasses, according to the riches of His grace' (Ephesians 1:7).

> I am redeemed, O praise the Lord!
> My soul from bondage free
> Has found at last a resting-place
> In Him who died for me
>
> The debt is paid, my soul is free
> And by His mighty power
> The blood that washed my sins away
> Still cleanseth every hour
>
> I am redeemed! I am redeemed!
> I'll sing it o'er and o'er
> I am redeemed! O praise the Lord!
> Redeemed for evermore!
>
> Julia Sterling (1820–1915)

Divine
remission

Chapter 2

*I am writing to you, little children, because your sins
are forgiven for His sake.*

1 John 2:12

The above verse was written by an intimate of the Lord
Jesus Christ. It was written by John, '... the disciple
whom Jesus loved, who had lain close to His breast at the
[Lord's] supper' (John 21:20). But when John penned the
above verse, he was no longer the young man who had
followed the Saviour so closely while He was here on earth.
John was now advanced in years. He was by now an elder
statesman and a disciple of vast Christian experience.
Our verse, though, shows that he was keen to keep things
simple and stick to basics. John knew just how central the
forgiveness of sins was, and is, to the Christian faith and
to the soul's earthly and eternal well-being. And so, he
wrote to both assure and re-assure: 'I am writing to you,
little children, because your sins are forgiven for His sake.'

A basic fundamental

The forgiveness of sins '... for His sake' (1 John 2:12)—that
is, on account of who Jesus is and what He has done—is
both a basic fundamental of the Christian faith and a
blessing peculiar to the Christian faith. It is unique to
the Christian faith and it could not be more vital. Why?
Because to die unforgiven is to die eternally condemned
by God. But if our sins are forgiven, we are eternally right
with God and heirs of His Kingdom. Divine remission is

therefore a basic of Christian salvation. The *Apostles'
Creed* saw fit to include the line, 'I believe in ... the
forgiveness of sins'[1], in its concise summary of Christian
essentials. Likewise, no less a colossus than John Calvin
once wrote:

> It is on the foundation of the remission of sins that
> our salvation is built and stands. This remission
> is, in fact, the door to approaching God and the
> instrument which holds and keeps us in His
> kingdom.

Christ has Himself purchased the remission of sins
and paid for it with the price of His own blood, so that we
might have it without paying anything. It is in this blood
alone that we must seek for cleansing from our sins and
for redress for them.[2]

An explanation and exploration

What exactly, though, did John have in mind here when,
under the guidance of the Holy Spirit, he assured his
readers, '... your sins are forgiven for His sake' (1 John
2:12)? The verb, *to forgive*, which John employs here means
to cancel or remit. To paraphrase, we could say, 'Your sins
are cancelled because Jesus has wiped them out.' John is
saying that the dreadful debt we owe to God—the penalty
for our sins—has been paid for by the Lord Jesus Christ
when He died for our sins on the cross. Jesus intervened
and paid what we owed in our stead when He was '...

offered once to bear the sins of many' (Hebrews 9:28). It was the logic and *theologic* of this which caused Augustus Toplady (1740–78) to compose the following lines—lines which rejoice in the payment of eternal validity that Christ made when He died on the cross, and lines which consequently help banish any doubts the believer may have in relation to his or her eternal security:

> From whence this fear and unbelief
> Hath not the Father put to grief
> His spotless Son for me?
> And will the righteous Judge of men
> Condemn me for that debt of sin
> Which Lord, was charged on Thee?
>
> Complete atonement Thou hast made
> And to the utmost Thou hast paid
> Whate'er Thy people owed
> How then can wrath on me take place
> If sheltered in Thy righteousness
> And sprinkled with Thy blood?
>
> If Thou hast my discharge procured
> And freely in my room endured
> The whole of wrath divine
> Payment God cannot twice demand
> First at my bleeding Surety's hand
> And then again at mine.

Secondly, the verb *to forgive,* which John employed, can also be translated *to send away.* To paraphrase again then, we could say, 'Your sins have all been sent away through the work and achievement of the Lord Jesus Christ.' Hebrews 9:26 likewise affirms, 'He has appeared once for all at the end of the age to put away sin by the sacrifice of Himself.'

It is the sacrifice of the Lord Jesus on Calvary, therefore, which puts the sins that condemn us far out of God's sight. Later in 1 John, he wrote, 'You know that He appeared to take away sins, and in Him there is no sin' (1 John 3:5). Perhaps John had the *scapegoat* imagery of Old Testament times in mind when he wrote this. On the Day of Atonement, the high priest used to confess the peoples' sins over the head of a live goat, symbolically transferring them onto it. The stipulation then was to 'send him away into the wilderness ... The goat shall bear all their iniquities upon him to a solitary land' (Leviticus 16:21, 22). It was all a picture of the Christ to come—an Old Testament foreshadowing of New Testament realities. The gospel proclaims that Jesus is the One who takes all our sins away! 'Behold, the Lamb of God, who takes away the sin of the world' (John 1:29). If our faith is in Him, our sins are cancelled. If our faith is in Him our sins are removed from God's sight. 'As far as the east is from the west, so far does He remove our transgressions from us' (Psalm 103:12).

Divine remission is a Christian basic, integral to salvation. It is the Christian gospel. 'There is therefore now no condemnation for those who are in Christ Jesus' (Romans 8:1). Central to the Christian faith is the forgiveness of sins—a forgiveness wrought by the death of Christ for our sins on the cross. So, if your faith is in the crucified Saviour, the Bible assures you that, '... your sins are forgiven for His sake' (1 John 2:12).

Divine justification

Chapter 3

Justified by His blood.

Romans 5:9

It would seem that the apostle Paul's favourite way of elucidating Christian salvation was by using the term *justification*. His largest letter in the New Testament—the epistle to the Romans—is a systematic explanation and exposition of the doctrine of the divine justification of the one who puts his or her faith in Christ. Paul's gospel was the gospel of justification. From various angles, Paul explains: '... we are now justified by His blood' (Romans 5:9); we are '... justified by His grace as a gift' (Romans 3:24); we are '... justified by faith' (Romans 5:1); and 'It is God who justifies' (Romans 8:33). In summary, God—Paul states—'... justifies him who has faith in Jesus' (Romans 3:26).

Prior to this, in the shorter epistle to the Galatians—possibly Paul's earliest letter—Paul took up controversially what he later explained in Romans systematically. Justification by God's grace alone, through faith alone, in Christ alone, was under threat in the province of Galatia. There was a false gospel of justification by human works being peddled in the area. Paul reacted by taking up his pen to defend the doctrine of divine justification. His language in Galatians is strong. In Galatians 2:16 Paul is contending for the true faith stating, '... that a man is not justified by works of the law, but through faith in Jesus Christ'.

What is justification all about?

What exactly do we mean by divine justification? The word is part of the Christian vocabulary and the New Testament mindset, but not really in common use today. Our word processors have the facility to *justify* text—that is, to adjust lines neatly to the right—but this is not what we are dealing with here. A good and precise definition is called for, and the *Shorter Catechism's* definition is difficult to better. In answer to the question 'What is justification?' it states:

> Justification is an act of God's free grace, wherein He pardoneth all our sins and accepteth us as righteous in His sight, only for the righteousness of Christ imputed to us and received by faith alone.[1]

Lawson comments on this as follows:

> Justification means pronouncing a person righteous; it is the opposite of condemnation. It is said to be an act because it is done at once; and an act of God's free grace because we can do nothing of ourselves to deserve it. It consists of two parts— pardon and acceptance; and we are taught also that the cause of it is not our own goodness, but Christ's, and that Christ's righteousness becomes ours through faith.[2]

Justification concerns the most vital matter of all: being rightly related to God our Maker. Justification concerns being right with God. If we are rightly related to God, all is eternally well with our souls.

The verdict: Guilty!

The nub of the problem is that by nature we are not rightly related to God, and we are not rightly related to God because we are sinners by nature and practice. The Scripture's diagnosis of us all, without exception, is, 'None is righteous, no, not one' (Romans 3:10). 'Since all have sinned and fall short of the glory of God' (Romans 3:23). It is our sin which makes us *not right* with God. It is our unrighteousness which necessitates being accounted righteous before Him.

The doctrine of justification takes us into the realms of the law courts. A judge has the power to pronounce 'Guilty' or 'Not guilty'. Sadly, at God's bar, we are all pronounced 'Guilty'. We have all broken God's law and thus, His terrible sentence—eternal punishment—hangs over us. It is against the law of God that the guilty verdict is announced, '... that every mouth may be stopped, and the whole world may be held accountable to God ... since through the law comes knowledge of sin' (Romans 3:19, 20).

The verdict: Not Guilty!

The wonder of the Christian gospel, however, is the wonder of divine justification—the divine declaration of the sinner as 'Not guilty'. The gospel proclaims that guilty sinners may be acquitted—they may be declared righteous in God's sight and be declared righteous before Him for all eternity. How can this ever be? The Bible's answer is this: *through the saving grace of God in His Son, the Lord Jesus Christ.* Or, to quote Romans, '... through faith in Jesus Christ for all who believe' (Romans 3:22).

Love and Justice: Justice and Love

Jesus came into the world so that condemned sinners could be acquitted, and acquitted without compromising God's justice. On the cross of Calvary, He *served the sentence* of all who believe in Him. Jesus was reckoned a guilty sinner, so that, by faith in Him, guilty sinners may be declared not guilty. It can only be explained by the grace of God—His unmerited favour and undeserved kindness to guilty sinners. It can only be explained by the mercy of God—He has spared the believer because He did not spare His own Son. To quote one of Paul's fullest statements on justification—how a guilty sinner is declared righteous before God:

> They are justified by His grace as a gift, through the redemption which is in Christ Jesus, whom God put forward as an expiation by His blood, to be received by faith. This was to show God's righteousness, because in His divine forbearance He had passed over former sins; it was to prove at the present time

that He Himself is righteous and that He justifies him who has faith in Jesus (Romans 3:24–26).

Why the cross?

The doctrine of divine justification, and the Christian's experience of divine justification cannot be divorced from the cross of Christ and the Christ of the cross. At Calvary, Jesus was punished so that sinners could be pardoned. At Calvary, Jesus was treated as guilty so that sinners could be declared 'not guilty', and 'not guilty' forever. Romans 5:1 affirms, 'Therefore, since we are justified by faith, we have peace with God through our Lord Jesus Christ.'

The great revival of the doctrine

This precious doctrine of divine justification came to the forefront at the Protestant Reformation of the sixteenth century. The treasure had lain buried for centuries, but was unearthed again by Martin Luther, when he discovered and rediscovered the message of Romans. Romans teaches that the righteousness we need to be right with God is a righteousness which God actually freely gives us, through Christ, His Son. It is not something to be earned but something to be received—by faith. To quote Luther's own testimony:

> I greatly longed to understand Paul's epistle to the Romans ... I grasped that the justice of God is that righteousness by which, through grace and sheer

> mercy, God justifies us through faith. Thereupon I
> felt myself to be reborn and to have gone through
> open doors into paradise ... it became to me
> inexpressibly sweet ... a gate to heaven.[3]

It was the rediscovery of the message of the gospel of divine justification which triggered the Protestant Reformation. The Protestant Reformation proved to be the greatest revival of biblical Christianity since the days of the apostles. Its legacy is still with us today.

Divine Justification: God's Gospel

Thank God for the truth of divine justification—that salvation is by His grace alone, in the Christ of Calvary alone, received by faith alone. This was the faith of Martin Luther. This was the faith of the apostle Paul. The justification of the sinner was the reason for Christ's mission from heaven to earth and justification by divine mercy, not human merit, was taught clearly by the Master Himself. Jesus once told a parable about a 'good' man who went to hell and a 'bad' man who went to heaven. The 'good' man tried to gain heaven by his own works and respectability. He failed. The 'bad' man, though, cast himself solely on the mercy of God and prayed, 'God be merciful to me a sinner!' (Luke 18:13). The final outcome, Jesus said, was, 'This man went down to his house *justified* [right with God] rather than the other; for every one who exalts himself will be humbled, but he who humbles himself will be exalted' (Luke 18:14).

Divine adoption

Chapter 4

See what love the Father has given us, that we should
be called children of God; and so we are.

1 John 3:1

In considering divine adoption, we are considering one of the Christian's highest and greatest of blessings. Amazingly, a Christian is one who, by God's grace in Christ, has been taken into God's family, and is consequently able to know, love and address God as 'Father', secure under His love for all eternity. You could say that it is almost too good and too staggering to be true! But the Bible tells us so. The word John uses in the above verse to describe the adopting love of God can be translated as 'from another country'. John is saying that the saving love of God is absolutely heavenly. It is truly *out of this world*. Here is a blessing to enjoy. Here is a salvation to celebrate. Here is fuel for wonder and praise:

Behold, what love, what boundless love
The Father hath bestowed
On sinners lost, that we should be
Now called the sons of God

No longer far from Him, but now
By 'precious blood' made nigh
Accepted in the 'Well-beloved'
Near to God's heart we lie.

Anonymous

Taken into the family

What is a Christian? A Christian is a child of God. Christians collectively constitute, 'the household [or family] of God' (1 Timothy 3:15). A Christian knows God as Father and submits to His loving authority and basks in His loving affection. Christians collectively pray to God with the words, 'Our Father, who art in heaven'. But how is it that Christians are to be considered as the privileged children of God? Solely by the grace of God. Solely by virtue of their divine adoption. They did not always possess their high status, but there came a moment in their lives, planned by God in eternity past, when He intervened in saving grace. When did the Christian's adoption occur? When they were enabled to receive Christ as their own personal Saviour. Our sonship derives from His Sonship. We are adopted into God's family through Him. 'But to all who received Him, who believed in His name, He gave power to become children of God; who were born, not of blood nor of the will of the flesh nor of the will of man, but of God' (John 1:12, 13). We are all born into a human family. But not everyone is born again into the divine family: Christians are! Such people, whatever their lot in this life, have reason to count themselves as the dearest and the blessed!

Let us now consider this saving blessing a little more precisely. The *Shorter Catechism* numbers adoption as one of the benefits of salvation. It asks the question, 'What is adoption?' Its answer is well worth weighing:

> Adoption is an act of God's free grace, whereby we are received into the number and have a right to all the privileges of the sons of God.[1]

Lawson's comment unpacks this concise definition very helpfully when he explains:

> Adoption denotes the taking of a child, who is a stranger, into a family and treating him as a member of it. Such is the adoption meant here. It … is an act of pure favour on God's part and confers blessings to which we had lost all claim. It confers upon us both the rank and rights of children, and makes us feel that we have both a place and a portion as sons in God's family.[2]

The *Westminster Confession of Faith*'s unfolding of divine adoption is fuller. It mentions its blessings not only in relation to this life but also in relation to the life to come. It states:

> All those that are justified, God vouchsafeth in and for His only Son Jesus Christ, to make partakers of the grace of adoption, by which they are taken into the number and enjoy the liberties and privileges of the children of God, have His name put upon them, receive the spirit of adoption, have access to the throne of grace with boldness, are enabled to cry Abba, Father, are pitied, protected, provided for

and chastened by Him as by a Father: yet never cast off, but sealed to the day of redemption; and inherit the promises as heirs of everlasting salvation.[3]

Meet Sally

We once had a pretty, little cat called Sally. Sally was one of a litter of six, found abandoned by a railway line. She was rescued and we adopted her—we took her into our home. There she began to thrive. She enjoyed free run of the house and garden, two meals a day plus titbits and a special place in our hearts and by our hearth. Not bad for an abandoned cat, born into danger from trains, the elements and other animals.

Sally gives an illustration of what it is to be a Christian. We are all born spiritually hopeless, helpless and in danger. We are born sinners, '... so we were by nature children of wrath, like the rest of mankind' (Ephesians 2:3). But God, in Christ, intervened in saving grace. In Christ He both rescues us and adopts us into His family, and one day He will give us free run of His glorious home! Adoption has both present and promised blessings.

But when the time had fully come, God sent forth His Son, born of woman, born under the law, to redeem those who were under the law, so that we might receive adoption as sons. And because you are sons, God has sent the Spirit of His Son into our hearts, crying 'Abba! Father!' So through God you

38

are no longer a slave but a son, and if a son then an heir (Galatians 4:4–7).

Normal Christian testimony, then, is anything but normal. It may be tabulated like this:

- Born a child of wrath. Saved from the wrath of God by Jesus and His death on the cross. 'The Son of man came to seek and to save the lost' (Luke 19:10).
- Adopted into God's family. Safe under His providential care, day by day. An heir of the glorious kingdom of heaven ...

Such is divine adoption! It is a reality to rejoice in and value so much more than the passing things and matters of this life. Truth be told, if you are a Christian, and understand and know the blessing of divine adoption, you will not wish to exchange places with anyone else in the entire world.

O how shall I the goodness tell
Father, which thou to me hast showed?
That I, a child of wrath and hell
I should be called a child of God
Should know, should feel my sins forgiven
Blest with this antepast of heaven.

Charles Wesley (1707–88)

39

Divine regeneration

And you He made alive, when you were dead through the trespasses and sins in which you once walked.

Ephesians 2:1–2

The question is raised: If believing in Jesus is so crucial and vital for our eternal salvation, why are so many people totally unconcerned about this matter? The answer of the Bible is this: *because they are spiritually dead.* That is, they are alive physically—eating, drinking, breathing etc—but dead spiritually. And those in a state of spiritual deadness are, by their nature, incapable of saving faith in Christ, just as a physically dead person is incapable of breathing. The spiritually dead are spiritually dead! The spiritually dead are therefore oblivious to God, eternity, the perilous state of their souls and their need of Christ. Thus, for a spiritually dead person to believe in Jesus, they need to be made alive—they are in need of a spiritual regeneration. As only God Himself can give life, they are in need of *divine regeneration.*

Religious but dead!

Jesus Himself once explained to a highly religious and respectable man that his religion was not enough. He was in need of a spiritual rebirth. The man in question was one Nicodemus, a Pharisee. In solemn tones, Jesus explained to him—and also still says to us today—'Truly, truly, I say to you, unless one is born anew [literally 'from above'; that is, from God], he cannot see the kingdom of God' (John

3:3). Jesus was saying that if we are to enjoy fellowship with God, we need to be renewed from within—we need a spiritual rebirth. We need to be born again.

A work of God

Our chapter is headed *divine regeneration*. This has to be stressed, as spiritual regeneration is a work of God. We are as powerless to give ourselves the necessary spiritual rebirth, as we were powerless to conceive ourselves and give ourselves our physical birth. Divine regeneration reminds us that salvation is all *of God* from beginning to end—its decision, conception, accomplishment, reception and consummation. When it comes to our spiritual regeneration, we are totally passive. All this, of course, is very humbling to the human pride which says, 'I am the master of my fate: I am the captain of my soul.'[1] There is a mystery about the spiritual birth, just as there is a mystery about physical birth. 'As you do not know how the spirit comes to the bones in the womb of a woman with child, so you do not know the work of God who makes everything' (Ecclesiastes 11:5).

The new birth is a result of the working of the Spirit of God in our hearts. Yet we can no more control how the Spirit of God works than we can control how the wind blows. Jesus Himself went on to explain to Nicodemus, 'The wind blows where it wills, and you hear the sound of it, but you do not know whence it comes or whither it goes; so it is with every one who is born of the Spirit' (John 3:8).

Divine regeneration thus marks the very beginning of salvation in individual human experience. As a creative and re-creative work of God, we are purely passive in its operation. We do not *co-operate* with God to impart new life to ourselves! The new birth is, of course, difficult to explain. It can only really be known by its effects. Life itself cannot be explained fully, but the signs of life can be evidenced. This is so in the spiritual realm: a person is now alive to God; a person is aware of their sinful condition; a person hears the gospel of Christ with *new ears* and it makes compelling sense; a person is drawn to Christ and enabled to put their faith in Him. 'This effectual call is of God's free and special grace alone, not from anything at all foreseen in man, who is altogether passive therein, until, being quickened and renewed by the Holy Spirit, he is thereby enabled to answer this call, and to embrace the grace offered and conveyed in it' (*Westminster Confession*).[2]

Regeneration defined

For conciseness, it will now be helpful to quote from Louis Berkhof's *Systematic Theology* to further clarify what we mean by divine regeneration. Regeneration, he says, designates:

> That divine act by which the sinner is endowed with

new spiritual life, and by which the principle of that new life is first called into action ... Regeneration consists in the implanting of the principle of new spiritual life in man, in a radical change of the governing disposition of the soul, which, under the influence of the Holy Spirit, gives birth to a life that moves in a God-ward direction ... It is a secret and inscrutable work of God ... and can only be perceived by its effects. Regeneration is that act of God by which the principle of the new life is implanted in man, and the governing disposition of the soul is made holy.[3]

So, our sinful state is such that we are spiritually dead. 'A natural man ... being ... dead in sin, is not able by his own strength to convert himself or to prepare himself thereunto' (*Westminster Confession*).[4] But thank God that, what we are unable to do ourselves, by His grace, He does for us. How? Normally through the preaching of the gospel. The Holy Spirit works through means. The Holy Spirit works through the Word. Hence, Peter was not being contradictory when he wrote 'You have been born anew, not of perishable seed but of imperishable, through the living and abiding word of God' (1 Peter 1:23). It is through the preaching of the Word that God works, and calls us effectually:

... out of that state of sin and death, in which they are by nature, to grace and salvation, by Jesus

Christ; enlightening their minds spiritually and savingly to understand the things of God; taking away their heart of stone and giving unto them an heart of flesh; renewing their wills, and, by His almighty power, determining them to that which is good, and effectually drawing them to Jesus Christ: yet so, as they come most freely, being made willing by His grace (*Westminster Confession*).[5]

New life!

Christian conversion then—a change of life—is a result of the new birth. Saving faith in Christ—'an interest in the Saviour's blood' (Charles Wesley 1757–1834)—does not and cannot occur apart from a previous divine regeneration—the work of God's Spirit in convicting us of our sins and enabling us to realise both our need of Christ and the Christ for our need. Saving faith in Christ is not the cause but the result of divine regeneration.

Thank God then for divine regeneration: His intervention in our lives in saving grace. It was this which the Ephesians had experienced. Paul reminded them, 'And you He made alive, when you were dead. ... Even when we were dead through our trespasses, [God] made us alive together with Christ' (Ephesians 2:1, 5). And this experience is also common to every Christian. 'He saved us ... by the washing of regeneration and renewal in the Holy Spirit' (Titus 3:5).

45

We sometimes hear the expression, 'a born-again Christian'. Truth be told, this is a tautology—akin to a round circle, wet water and sweet sugar—for every true Christian has been born again. We become a Christian not at birth but at our rebirth. Saving faith in Christ is the result, not the cause of divine regeneration. Thus, if we do not have saving faith in Christ, we need to heed the Saviour's famous words 'You must be born anew' (John 3:7).

> A ruler once came to Jesus by night
> To ask Him the way of salvation and light;
> The Master made answer in words true and plain,
> 'Ye must be born again.'
>
> Ye children of men, attend to the word
> So solemnly uttered by Jesus the Lord;
> And let not this message to you be in vain,
> 'Ye must be born again.'
>
> O ye who would enter that glorious rest,
> And sing with the ransomed the song of the blest,
> The life everlasting if ye would obtain,
> 'Ye must be born again.'
>
> *'Ye must be born again!'*
> *I verily, verily, say unto thee*
> *'Ye must be born again!'*

Divine
purification

Chapter 6

The blood of Jesus, His Son, cleanses us from all sin.

1 John 1:7

Cleansing for the soul

Martin Luther, the great Reformer, allegedly used to say words to the effect that, 'There are only two sacraments, the bread and the bath.' Both of these point us to the death of Christ at Calvary, and the blessings that flow from it. By 'the bath', Luther was referring, of course, to Christian baptism.

What is Christian baptism? The *Shorter Catechism* defines it so:

> Baptism is a sacrament, wherein the *washing with water*, in the name of the Father and of the Son and of the Holy Ghost, doth signify and seal our ingrafting into Christ and partaking of the benefits of the Covenant of Grace, and our engagement to be the Lord's.[1]

Note those words in italics: *the washing with water*. Salvation is not tied to physical baptism—the dying thief went to Paradise and was never baptised—yet salvation, according to the Bible, entails a spiritual washing, a cleansing of the soul, a cleansing of which water baptism is a sign. Lawson's comment on the significance of baptism is helpful:

> The outward act in baptism is washing with water in the name of the Father, and of the Son and of

the Holy Ghost. The inward meaning of this is the removal of our sin ... the baptismal fountain of water tells us of another fountain, which is filled with the blood of Jesus Christ, and which has been opened freely for all sin and uncleanness.[2]

Back to the cross

When Jesus died at Calvary, John records, 'One of the soldiers pierced His side with a spear, and at once there came out blood and water' (John 19:34). Physically, this was due to the puncturing of the Saviour's pericardium—the sack which surrounds the heart. But John records this more for its spiritual significance. The blood speaks of sacrifice. 'Without the shedding of blood there is no forgiveness of sins' (Hebrews 9:22). The water however speaks of purification. Both of these are necessary for the sinner's salvation. Purification—divine purification—is one of the Bible's lesser-known metaphors used to depict salvation. Divine purification is another way in which the Bible depicts the *blessing of all blessings*, and divine purification is also the theme of many gospel hymns. By faith we wash in the blood of Jesus, and in doing so our sins are washed away and we are made fit for God's presence:

> There is a fountain filled with blood
> Drawn from Immanuel's veins;
> And sinners, plunged beneath that flood,
> Lose all their guilty stains.

The dying thief rejoiced to see
That fountain in his day;
And there may I, though vile as he,
Wash all my sins away.

William Cowper (1731–1800)

The necessity for purification

Purification—that is, cleansing—therefore, is another way in which the Bible depicts the blessing of salvation. Again though, the bad news is the necessary backcloth to the good. The bad news is that we are in desperate need of cleansing if we are to be saved, and we are so because we are sinners by nature and practice. The Bible depicts sin as a state of moral defilement that renders us unfit for God's holy presence, and even abhorrent to Him. The God of the universe is a God '... of purer eyes than to behold evil and canst not look on wrong' (Habakkuk 1:13). It is written of the New Jerusalem—the Kingdom of heaven—that '... nothing unclean shall enter it' (Revelation 21:27), and Scripture teaches that by nature we are unclean.

There is a city bright
Closed are its gates to sin
Naught that defileth
Naught that defileth
Can ever enter in.

Mary A. S. Deck (1813–1903)

51

Paradoxically, Scripture teaches that we need to be purified as much because of God's holiness as we do because of our sin. Scripture states that, 'God is light and in Him is no darkness at all' (1 John 1:5). God's holiness and our sin are incompatible. A facet of God's holiness is His immaculate and indescribable moral purity, which finds sin totally repugnant to His nature. Whilst Almighty God can do anything, He is incapable of changing His nature. He cannot cease from being holy, for He cannot cease from being God. Eliphaz, one of Job's 'comforters' was not always tactful or compassionate. But he uttered the truth when he said, 'What is man, that he can be clean? Or he that is born of woman, that he can be righteous? Behold, God puts no trust in His holy ones, and the heavens are not clean in His sight; how much less one who is abominable and corrupt, a man who drinks iniquity like water!' (Job 15:14–16).

It is the testimony of both Scripture and human experience that the nearer we get to God, the more we become aware of our inner uncleanness. His light exposes our darkness. His incredible purity exposes our impurity. Against the light of God, even our supposed goodness is revealed to be tainted and stained by sin. Isaiah wrote, 'We have all become like one who is unclean, and all our righteous deeds are like a polluted garment' (Isaiah 64:6). Isaiah received his call to his prophetic ministry subsequent to being given a glimpse of God's sovereignty, purity and glory. He witnessed God on His throne, and the seraphim saying, 'Holy, holy, holy is the LORD of hosts; the whole earth is full of His glory' (Isaiah 6:3). It was God's holiness which convicted Isaiah of his sin and his need for cleansing. He cried out, 'Woe is me! For I am lost; for I am a man of unclean lips, and I dwell in the midst of a people of unclean lips; for my eyes have seen the King, the LORD of hosts!' (Isaiah 6:5).

We began this chapter with a reference to Martin Luther the great Reformer. Another one of Luther's alleged statements was this: 'The recognition of sin is the beginning of salvation.'[3] He was absolutely right. We will only be concerned about seeking divine purification if we sense our deep need for it. The Holy Spirit of God alone can truly convict and convince us of our unfitness for God's presence and our need to be cleansed from our sin. We realise that the remedy does not lie in ourselves. With David we turn to God for mercy and say, 'Wash me thoroughly from my iniquity and cleanse me from my sin' (Psalm 51:2). Salvation thus begins in our personal experience when we realise—or are enabled to realise—that because of who God is and because of who we are, we need to be cleansed from our sin. 'Who can say, "I have made my heart clean; I am pure from my sin"?' (Proverbs 20:9):

> Eternal Light! Eternal Light!
> How pure the soul must be
> When, placed within Thy searching sight,

It shrinks not, but with calm delight
Can live and look on Thee.

Thomas Binney (1789–1874)

The glory of the gospel, however, is that the necessity for cleansing has been met by the grace and mercy of God in Christ. In Old Testament times, God promised, 'I will sprinkle clean water upon you, and you shall be clean from all your uncleannesses, and from all your idols I will cleanse you' (Ezekiel 36:25). In Old Testament times, God foretold of '… a fountain opened … to cleanse them from sin and uncleanness' (Zechariah 13:1). In Old Testament times, God promised 'Come now, let us reason together, says the LORD: though your sins are like scarlet, they shall be as white as snow; though they are red like crimson, they shall become like wool' (Isaiah 1:18). These divine promises ultimately find their divine fulfilment in Christ. In Christ, God has provided the necessary cleansing from sin for all who turn to Him and avail themselves of God's provision.

The provision of purification

1 John 1:7 contains the glorious affirmation: 'The blood of Jesus His Son cleanses us from all sin.' The very verb which the Holy Spirit employs for 'cleanses' or 'purifies' here is in the present continuous tense. It tells us that the blood of Jesus, shed at Calvary, carries on cleansing us from all sin. It tells us that the sacrifice which Christ freely offered

at Calvary is a sacrifice of eternal validity to all who avail themselves of it by faith.

According to the Bible then, salvation entails a divine purification. It is the gospel. God in Christ has provided the needed washing for souls which are defiled and soiled by sin. In a lengthy, yet compact statement concerning salvation, Paul explains in Titus 3:4–7:

> When the goodness and loving kindness of God our Saviour appeared, He saved us, not because of deeds done by us in righteousness, but in virtue of His own mercy, by the washing of regeneration and renewal in the Holy Spirit, which He poured out upon us richly through Jesus Christ our Saviour, so that we might be justified by His grace and become heirs in hope of eternal life.

The reality of purification

But does the blood of Jesus really wash away our sins and make us fit for glory? The answer to this may be gleaned if we read John the apostle's inspired and privileged *glimpse of the glory* in Revelation 7. John was enabled to see, '... a great multitude which no man could number ... standing before the throne and before the Lamb ... crying out with a loud voice' (Revelation 7:9, 10). The question was raised: 'Who are these, clothed in white robes, and whence have they come?' (Revelation 7:13). And the answer was given: 'These are they who have come out of the great tribulation; *they have washed their robes and made them white in the blood of the Lamb. Therefore are they before the throne of God and serve Him day and night within His temple ...*' (Revelation 7:14, 15). We see here that the soul-cleansing blood of Jesus alone is the sinner's passport to God's nearer presence.

The glories of heaven, God's dwelling place, therefore, are not the prerogative of all, but only those who, by God's grace, know a divine purification from their sins—specifically those who, '... have washed their robes and made them white in the blood of the Lamb' (Revelation 7:14). The evangelistic thrust of the Christian faith therefore is simple: 'Wash, and be clean' (2 Kings 5:13)—that is, avail yourself of God's provision in Christ for the sinner's cleansing.

How vital it is, therefore, to know the divine purification we have just considered, if we are ever to be saved. Jesus' words to Peter have a wider application than when they were first uttered: 'If I do not wash you, you have no part in me' (John 13:8). The gospel of Christ is a divine purification—God's gracious provision to enable unclean sinners to be cleansed from their sin and made fit for His holy presence. 1 John 1:7 again states in all its simplicity and profundity: 'The blood of Jesus His Son cleanses us from all sin.' It begs the most important question of all:

> Have you been to Jesus for the cleansing power?
> Are you washed in the blood of the Lamb?

Are you fully trusting in His grace this hour
Are you washed in the blood of the Lamb?

Lay aside the garments that are stained with sin,
And be washed in the blood of the Lamb;
There's a fountain flowing for the soul unclean,
O be washed in the blood of the Lamb!

Are you washed in the blood,
In the soul-cleansing blood of the Lamb?
Are your garments spotless? Are they white as snow?
Are you washed in the blood of the Lamb?

Elisha Albright Hoffman (1839–1929)

Divine propitiation

Chapter 7

He [the Lord Jesus] is the propitiation for our sins.

1 John 2:2, NKJV

Although the word 'propitiation' above—the Greek word is 'hilasmos'—is not a word we use in general everyday use, *propitiation* is absolutely central to the Christian doctrine and experience of salvation. Propitiation lies at the heart of the Christian gospel and—not to put it too strongly—if we have failed to understand the cross of Christ as an act of divine propitiation, we have failed to understand the meaning of the cross of Christ at all.

Definitions

If propitiation is so crucial to Christian salvation, what exactly do we mean—and what exactly does the Bible mean—when it uses the word? The verb, *to propitiate,* means *to appease.* It means *to turn aside the anger.* It means *to satisfy* and *gain the forgiveness or favour of.* So, when the Bible refers to the saving work of Christ as an act of propitiation, it is saying that the Lord Jesus Christ, by His death on the cross for our sins, has turned aside the wrath of God, which the believer deserved for their sins. The doctrine of propitiation proclaims that Jesus has won our peace with God, because He has paid the penalty for our sins and satisfied the just anger of God for our sins. The Bible tells of His '... making peace by the blood of His cross' (Colossians 1:20). Thus, propitiation is integral to the blessed atonement which all believers enjoy, having put their faith in the crucified Christ:

> The wrath of God that was our due,
> Upon the Lamb was laid;
> And by the shedding of His blood,
> The debt for us was paid.
>
> D. W. Whittle (1840–1901)

The unpopular truth

Divine propitiation lies at the heart of Calvary. The doctrine, however, is not often preached today because, behind it all, there underlies a reality which many would prefer to shy away from, namely the fearful and formidable reality of the wrath of God. The 'God' which many believe in today is a god of their own imagination and liking, who is indifferent to sin. The 'God' which is widely proclaimed today is a god who is a 'tolerant' god, who supposedly loves everyone, no matter what they believe or how they behave. This 'God' does not react at all when people fail to give Him the honour and obedience which is His due, or blatantly flout His commandments, and proudly live a lifestyle condemned in His Word. The 'God' widely propagated by our media today is the 'God' mentioned in Malachi 2:17: 'Every one who does evil is good in the sight of the Lord, and He delights in them.' The 'God' which this world believes in—if they believe in anything at all—is an apathetic 'God'. They 'say in their hearts, "The Lord will not do good, nor will He do ill"' (Zephaniah 1:12). But how infinitely different is all this from the nature of the one true God who is revealed in the Bible.

The biblical doctrine of the wrath of God

In Nahum 1:2, 3 we read: 'The LORD is a jealous God and avenging, ... the LORD takes vengeance on His adversaries and keeps wrath for His enemies. The LORD is slow to anger and of great might, and the LORD will by no means clear the guilty.' Then in Ephesians 2:3 we are reminded that all of us are '... by nature children of wrath, like the rest of mankind'. We are 'sinners in the hands of an angry God' (Jonathan Edwards)[1]—born with a nature that naturally rebels against God and will have to suffer the damnable consequences of having such a nature, unless there is a way of salvation.

The *Heidelberg Catechism* clarifies all this when it asks and answers the following:

> Will God suffer such disobedience and apostasy to go unpunished?
>
> By no means, but He is terribly displeased with our inborn as well as our actual sins and will punish them in just judgment in time and eternity, as He has declared: Cursed is every one that continueth not in all things which are written in the book of the law to do them.

Is God not also merciful?

> God is indeed merciful, but He is likewise just, wherefore His justice requires that sin, which is committed against the most high majesty of God, be also punished with extreme, that is, with everlasting punishment, both of body and soul.[2]

So, the necessary backcloth to the gospel is the reality of the wrath of God against sin. Sin is an affront to God. Sin has to be punished by God. Sin will be punished by God. God's justice and wrath are as equally a part of His nature as His grace and goodness. Sin has to be punished—or justly pardoned, without compromising God's just nature. And it is here that the cross of Christ comes in.

The wonder of the gospel

Paradoxically, sinners may escape from the wrath of God by the love of God. God Himself has mercifully provided a way whereby we may be delivered from His wrath: 'He … did not spare His own Son but gave Him up for us all' (Romans 8:32).

In 1 John 4:10 [NKJV] we read, 'In this is love, not that we loved God but that He loved us and sent His Son to be the propitiation for our sins.' *Propitiation*—explicit here, and implicit throughout the Bible—is the one word which truly unlocks the meaning of the cross of Christ and the way of salvation. Sin has to be punished by God, either in the sinner or in a substitute who takes the place of the sinner. The gospel proclaims that Christ is that Substitute. The gospel proclaims, '... that Christ died for our sins in accordance with the Scriptures' (1 Corinthians 15:3). That is, Christ took the place of sinners at Calvary. He was punished for our sins so that we might know pardon for our sins. He was judged for our justification. He endured the wrath of God for our sins to save us from the wrath of God we deserve for our sins. 'Jesus ... delivers us from the wrath to come' (1 Thessalonians 1:10). 'For God has not destined us for wrath, but to obtain salvation through our Lord Jesus Christ' (1 Thessalonians 5:9). 'Since, therefore, we are now justified by His blood, much more shall we be saved by Him from the wrath of God' (Romans 5:9).

When Christ died at Calvary, Scripture reports that, 'From the sixth hour there was darkness over all the land until the ninth hour' (Matthew 27:45). Why? Because He was enduring the wrath of God in our place. He was going through the 'outer darkness' (Matthew 22:13) of hell itself, the ultimate in God's wrath. When Christ died at Calvary, He cried out, 'My God, my God, why hast Thou forsaken Me?' (Matthew 27:46). Why? He was forsaken by God to procure our forgiveness from God. Jesus suffered the divine anger so that we could know the divine atonement. His death was propitiation. His death turned aside the wrath of God due to us. 'He is the propitiation for our sins' (1 John 2:2) [NKJV]. And if we belong to Jesus, we will be eternally grateful that this is so.

Jehovah lifted up His rod,
O Christ, it fell on Thee!
Thou wast sore stricken of Thy God;
There's not one stroke for me.
Thy tears, Thy blood beneath it flowed;
Thy bruising healeth me.

Jehovah bade His sword awake,
O Christ, it woke 'gainst Thee!
Thy blood the flaming blade must slake;
Thy heart its sheath must be—
All for my sake, my peace to make;
Now sleeps that sword for me.

Anne Ross Cousin (1824–1906)

Divine reconciliation

We ... rejoice in God through our Lord Jesus Christ, through whom we have now received our reconciliation.

Romans 5:11

Accord to the apostle Paul, the message of the gospel and 'the message of reconciliation' (2 Corinthians 5:19) are one and the same. Hence, the imperative of the gospel is to believe it and so '... be reconciled to God' (2 Corinthians 5:20). With this, the apostle Peter concurs. Christ's death, says Peter, was not pointless but purposeful. Reconciliation was its distinct aim and purpose: 'For Christ also died for sins once for all, the righteous for the unrighteous, that He might bring us to God' (1 Peter 3:18). *Reconciliation* is therefore a key and clue word and experience in the vocabulary of salvation. But what exactly do we mean by reconciliation?

Definitions

The verb, *to reconcile*, means *to bring together two parties when they have been estranged*. Reconciliation itself refers to the resultant state of harmony that exists between the two parties after they have been reconciled. The opposite of reconciliation is alienation. Alienation refers to an uncomfortable state of separation and estrangement between two parties—something has caused there to be a barrier and rift between them.

Reconciliation's necessity

The brightness of the Christian gospel of reconciliation makes no sense apart from the dark background of alienation. The bad news precedes the good. The diagnosis precedes the cure. The bad news is that we are sinners by nature and practice, and as such we are alienated from God—out of fellowship with Him. Scripture reveals that, 'God is light and in Him is no darkness at all' (1 John 1:5). He is '... of purer eyes than to behold evil and canst not look on wrong' (Habakkuk 1:13). God's indescribable holiness and our sin are incompatible. 'Your iniquities have made a separation between you and your God, and your sins have hid His face from you ...' (Isaiah 59:2). It is our sin which has to be dealt with if we are ever to be reconciled to God. It is our sin which has to be dealt with if we are ever to know fellowship with God and so realise our chief end of glorifying Him and enjoying Him forever. The message of the gospel is indeed *the message of reconciliation*. The bad news though is that we desperately need to be reconciled to God if all is to be eternally well with us.

You will notice that our chapter heading is *Divine* reconciliation. This is so because—in-line with our other chapter headings—the reconciliation integral to salvation is a work of God. The initiative is God's and not ours— technically known as *prevenient grace*. Reconciliation to

God is a result of God's gracious initiative and action in Christ, and not a result of any attempts we make to reform our lives and reconcile ourselves to God. In 2 Corinthians 5:19 Paul affirms that, 'In Christ, God was reconciling the world to Himself, not counting their trespasses against them.' The Greek which the Holy Spirit employs for 'in Christ' here is the *instrumental dative*. You could thus paraphrase it as 'God, by means of Christ, was reconciling the world to Himself ...'

The Mediator

The gospel of reconciliation is inextricably connected with Christ's office of Mediator. A mediator is a go-between. Industrial disputes are not unknown here in the UK. Sometimes a dispute between workers and management has been so great that the workers, on Union advice, have downed tools and gone out on strike, or taken industrial action. Production then comes to a grinding halt. In such an instance a mediator is employed—The Advisory, Conciliation and Arbitration Service (ACAS). Relations have broken off. Management is in one room. Union officials are in another. ACAS goes between the two and seeks conciliation and reconciliation. They discuss the cause of the dispute. They negotiate an agreement, perhaps a compromise. They shake hands and work begins again. ACAS have been able to negotiate a settlement.

In 1 Timothy 2:5 we read: 'There is one God and there

is one Mediator between God and men, the man Christ Jesus.' Jesus, the God-man is able to, as it were, take the hand of God and take our hand and bring us together—to reconcile us. He is the only Mediator between God and a sinful humanity. He is uniquely a Mediator in His Person— fully God and fully man—but He is especially uniquely the only 'Mediator between God and men' in His passion.

The reconciling cross

In the Bible, all roads lead to the cross of Calvary. This is especially so when we consider divine reconciliation. The reconciliation which Christians enjoy and celebrate was not achieved without a great cost, for it was achieved by Christ actually taking the cause of our separation from God on Himself and putting it away. It was achieved by His taking on Himself our sin. 'He Himself bore our sins in His body on the tree' (1 Peter 2:24). Or to quote 1 Peter 3:18 again: 'Christ also died for sins once for all, the righteous for the unrighteous, that He might bring us to God.'

We can see then that *reconciliation* and *atonement* are synonyms in the Christian vocabulary. It is Christ's death on the cross for our sins that has reconciled us to God—it has made us *at one*. It is Christ's death on the cross for our sins which has wrought our peace with God and even made the enemies of God His friends. 'While we were enemies we were reconciled to God by the death of His Son.' (Romans 5:10). 'Not only so, but we also rejoice in

God through our Lord Jesus Christ, through whom we have now received our reconciliation' (Romans 5:11). In the ancient tabernacle and temple, a curtain separated the holy of holies from the holy place. This graphically symbolised the separation between God and humanity. But when Christ died at Calvary, the Bible records that, 'The curtain of the temple was torn in two, from top to bottom' (Mark 15:38). Only a miracle explains this event. It was a direct act of God. It was His dramatic way of demonstrating that His Son's death really accomplishes the reconciliation of the believing sinner.

Divine reconciliation. It is the gospel which the church is obliged and mandated to proclaim. It is good news to receive. It is a salvation to celebrate. 'But now in Christ Jesus you who once were far off have been brought near in the blood of Christ' (Ephesians 2:13). Salvation is reconciliation. Salvation results in reconciliation— fellowship with God our Maker, for time and eternity. Thank God then, for the gospel of reconciliation—the work of God in bringing sinners to Himself.

A mind at perfect peace with God,
Oh! what a word is this!
A sinner reconciled through blood;
This, this indeed is peace!

By nature and by practice far,
How very far from God;

Yet now by grace brought nigh to Him,
Through faith in Jesus' blood.

So near, so very near to God,
I cannot nearer be;
For in the person of His Son
I am as near as He.

Horatius Bonar (1808–1889)

Divine
imputation

Chapter 9

*God was in Christ, reconciling the world unto Himself,
not imputing their trespasses unto them ...*

2 Corinthians 5:19, KJV

A lthough the word *imputation* is not really in common everyday use today, imputation actually lies at the heart of the Christian gospel and is a major key in understanding the exact nature of the cross-work of Christ and the salvation which accrues to the believer from it.

The word 'imputing' above is from the Greek verb, 'logizomai'. It means, *to count, reckon, credit or place to one's account.* The English word, *imputation,* contains the word, *put,* in it. So, while the word *imputation* is not in general use today, the concept is easily understood. You have a contract of employment which stipulates an agreed monthly salary. At the end of each month, a sum of money is credited to you—it is *put* to your account—for services rendered.

An awesome verse

In one of the profoundest verses in the Bible concerning the salvation Christ has won for His people at Calvary, 2 Corinthians 5:21 states: 'For our sake He made Him to be sin who knew no sin, so that in Him we might become the righteousness of God.' Divine imputation is central to this verse. It states that the cross of Christ was a saving transaction between Christ and the believer. It states that our sins were *imputed* to the sinless Christ, and it states that Christ's righteousness is actually *imputed* to us. We can therefore summarise that the blessed non-imputation of our sins to us, which is central to our salvation, has an objective basis. Its basis is that Christ has dealt with them. They were imputed to Him, as He was made to 'be sin' on our behalf, when He died as the sinner's substitute.

A visit to the bank
Divine imputation, then, views salvation using something of a banking metaphor. Our sins were imputed to Christ— He was made accountable for them. Negatively, He took our debt on Himself. Positively, Christ's righteousness is credited to our account. His righteousness is imputed to us, so that we are right with God for all eternity.

Scripture teaches that the believer's sins were imputed to Christ

'For our sake He made Him to be sin who knew no sin ...' (2 Corinthians 5:21). The unanimous testimony of the Bible is that Christ died in the sinner's place as the sinner's substitute. Death—physical and spiritual—is God's judgment on sin. Christ, however, alone of those born of woman, was totally sinless in His nature, and so could not and did not sin in either thought, word or deed. Thus, He was not subject to the penalty of sin, which is death. Yet on the cross, Christ died. His death was not for His own sins but for the sins of others. Our sins were *imputed* to

Him and He bore their consequence in our place: 'He was wounded for our transgressions; He was bruised for our iniquities' (Isaiah 53:5).

'Christ, having been offered once to bear the sins of many' (Hebrews 9:28).

'He Himself bore our sins in His body on the tree' (1 Peter 2:24).

'You know that He appeared to take away sins, and in Him there is no sin' (1 John 3:5).

Our sins were imputed to Christ at Calvary. Christ is '... the Lamb of God who takes away the sin of the world' (John 1:29). He is the reality and fulfilment behind the scapegoat of the Old Testament when all '... the iniquities of the people of Israel, and all their transgressions, all their sins ... he shall put them upon the head of the goat, and send him away into the wilderness ... The goat shall bear all their iniquities upon him ...' (Leviticus 16:21, 22).

So, Scripture teaches that the believer's sins were imputed to Christ. The substitutionary death of Christ is central to Christian salvation. Because our sins were imputed to Christ, they will not be imputed to us on the Judgment Day. Psalm 32:1–2 is the blessed portion of everyone who belongs to Jesus: 'Blessed is he whose transgression is forgiven, whose sin is covered. Blessed is the man to whom the LORD imputes no iniquity.'

> All thy sins were laid upon Him,
> Jesus bore them on the tree;

God who knew them, laid them on Him,

And, believing, thou art free.

Joseph Denham Smith (1816/17–1889)

Scripture teaches that the righteousness of Christ is imputed to the believer

In the Bible, the patriarch Abraham is very much viewed as *the father of the faithful*. Abraham was saved by the sheer grace of God. His faith was not in himself, but Godward. 'Abraham believed God, and it was reckoned to Him as righteousness' (Romans 4:3). Paul goes on to explain that the salvation of the believer is exactly the same: righteousness is not gained by graft, but given by grace, and as such is received by faith. 'And to one who does not work but trusts Him who justifies the ungodly, his faith is reckoned as righteousness' (Romans 4:5).

God made a promise to Abraham, and Abraham believed God's promise. Paul goes on to explain that Abraham was:

> … fully convinced that God was able to do what He had promised. That is why his faith was 'reckoned to him as righteousness'. But the words, 'it was reckoned to him', were written not for his sake alone, but for ours also. It will be reckoned to us who believe in Him that raised from the dead Jesus our Lord, who was put to death for our trespasses and raised for our justification (Romans 4:21–25).

Thus, the righteousness which saves us is not our own, intrinsic righteousness, but an *alien* one—the righteousness of Christ. He lived a sinless life and then gave us His life in an atoning sacrifice. All who put their faith in Him are credited with His perfect righteousness. This righteousness flows to us from the cross of Calvary. Salvation is a matter of being clothed with the perfect righteousness of Christ. It is imputed to the believer— received by faith. Every believer can make the words of Isaiah 61:10 their own: 'I will greatly rejoice in the LORD, my soul shall exult in my God; for He has clothed me with the garments of salvation, He has covered me with the robe of righteousness.' And it was the same for the apostle Paul. His religious past and present endeavours notwithstanding, his main desire was to be '... found in Him, not having a righteousness of my own, based on law, but that which is through faith in Christ, the righteousness from God that depends on faith' (Philippians 3:9).

> Jesus, Thy blood and righteousness
> My beauty are, my glorious dress;
> Midst flaming worlds, in these arrayed,
> With joy shall I lift up my head.
>
> John Wesley (1703–91)

So, *imputation* is indeed a key word of the gospel. Calvary was a saving transaction. Justification takes us to the law courts. Redemption takes us to the slave market. Adoption takes us to family matters. Imputation takes us to the world of accounting and banking—debit and credit. Our sin debt was imputed to Christ. His perfect righteousness is credited to us. It is the gospel of God—the gospel of divine imputation. 'For our sake He made Him to be sin who knew no sin, so that in Him we might become the righteousness of God' (2 Corinthians 5:21).

Divine
vocation

Chapter 10

My sheep hear my voice, and I know them, and they follow Me.

John 10:27

And those whom He predestined He also called ...

Romans 8:30

D id you know that it is as true to describe a Christian as one who has been *called by God* as it is to describe a Christian as one *redeemed by Christ, saved by grace* or *justified by faith* ? Christians are '... those who are *called* (Jude 1). Christians are '... holy brethren who share in a heavenly *call*' (Hebrews 3:1).

Divine vocation—the call of God in the gospel—is one of the vital links in the golden chain of salvation. The full verse of Romans 8:30 is very comprehensive. It begins in eternity past with God's eternal choice of His people for salvation, and ends in eternity future with their glorification—the consummation of their salvation. But. in between these eternal points, we see God's action in time. 'And those whom He predestined He also called; and those whom He called He also justified; and those whom He justified He also glorified' (Romans 8:30). The four major milestones in the Christian's salvation are enunciated here as follows:

1. Divine Predestination (or divine election)
2. Divine Vocation
3. Divine Justification
4. Divine Glorification.

Every one of these four golden links in the golden chain is vital for our eternal salvation. Here, though, we are concerned with the second link: divine vocation or divine calling.

The God who calls

When we talk about divine calling, we are talking about the application of divine salvation. We are affirming that those chosen by God for salvation in eternity past, will most certainly hear the call of the gospel in time, be enabled by God to respond to that call, and receive Christ and all His saving benefits. Almighty God will ensure that this is so. No natural or supernatural force will ever be able to prevent His elect from coming to saving faith in Christ, for Almighty God is as active in applying the work of salvation to His people as He was in planning their salvation and sending His Son to accomplish it. Salvation is a divine, not a human work. It is a case of a redemption divinely accomplished and divinely applied. If this were not so, none of us would ever come to know the joy of salvation. Jesus Himself said 'No one can come to Me unless the Father who sent Me draws him' (John 6:44).

Effectual calling

Another way in which divine vocation may be understood is by using the expression *effectual calling*. Effectual calling results in a sinner trusting the Saviour for salvation—but not before the Holy Spirit has convicted us of our sin and need of Christ, and enlightened us to the fact that Christ alone is the Saviour we desperately need. Effectual calling is the work of God's Holy Spirit. It is He who is God's agent of salvation in the world today. It is He who makes the way of salvation plain to us, draws us to Christ and nurtures in us saving faith in Him. The *Westminster Confession of Faith* has a full and pregnant statement concerning this when it states:

> All those whom God hath predestinated unto life, and those only, He is pleased, in His appointed and accepted time, effectually to call, by His Word and Spirit, out of that state of sin and death, in which they are by nature, to grace and salvation, by Jesus Christ; enlightening their minds spiritually and savingly to understand the things of God, taking away their heart of stone, and giving unto them an heart of flesh; renewing their wills, and by His almighty power, determining them to that which is good, and effectually drawing them to Jesus Christ: yet so, as they come most freely, being made willing by His grace.This effectual call is of God's free and special grace alone, not from anything at all foreseen in man, who is altogether passive therein, until, being quickened and renewed by the Holy

Spirit, he is thereby enabled to answer this call, and to embrace the grace offered and conveyed in it.[1]

The ordinary means of extraordinary grace

But how exactly does God call His elect to salvation in Christ? The answer is this: *in any way He sees fit*. God is sovereign in His operations. He might work through a providential crisis, when all our human props have been taken away from us. It might be through the testimony of a friend or a family member. It might be through reading a tract. God saves those from Christian backgrounds. God saves those from non-Christian backgrounds ... But the normal way of God's operation in calling His elect— both biblically and historically—seems to be through the preaching of the gospel. While we cannot dictate to the Almighty as to how His grace and call should come to anyone, His normal way of working is through means—the means of grace. And biblically and historically, His chief channel of grace is and has been the preaching of His Word:

> The Spirit of God maketh the reading, but especially the preaching of the Word, an effectual means of convincing and converting sinners and of building them up in holiness and comfort, through faith unto salvation (Shorter Catechism).[2]

Hence, in Romans 10:17, we read that, 'Faith comes from what is heard, and what is heard comes by the preaching of Christ.' Then, in Paul's first letter to the

Corinthians, he describes the Christians at Corinth as '... those sanctified in Christ Jesus, called to be saints ...' (1 Corinthians 1:2). And how did this call to salvation and sanctification come to them? Paul explained: 'It pleased God through the folly of what we preach to save those who believe' (1Corinthians 1:21). So, the Corinthian believers were who they were because they had heard and heeded the call of God in the gospel. The same was true of the believers in Thessalonica. Paul likewise explained to them that they were who they were because 'God chose you from the beginning to be saved, through sanctification by the Spirit and belief in the truth. To this He called you through our gospel' (2 Thessalonians 2:13, 14).

Conclusion

Divine calling, then, is integral to Christian salvation. Christians are who they are because they have heard and heeded the call of God in the gospel. Behind the voice of a fallible and flawed human preacher, they have perceived the clear voice of God. With hindsight, every Christian perceives that they have been a recipient and a beneficiary of ... *Divine Vocation.*

> I hear Thy welcome voice,
> That calls me Lord to Thee,
> For cleansing in Thy precious blood
> That flowed on Calvary.

Though coming weak and vile,
Thou dost my strength assure;
Thou dost my vileness fully cleanse,
Till spotless all and pure.

I am coming Lord!
Coming now to thee:
Wash me, cleanse me in the blood
That flowed on Calvary.

Lewis Hartsough (1828–1919)

And after you have suffered a little while, the God of all grace, who has called you to His eternal glory in Christ, will Himself restore, establish and strengthen you. To Him be the dominion for ever and ever. Amen (1 Peter 5:10, 11).

Divine
preservation

... and they shall never perish ...

John 10:28

The God who keeps

'The doctrine of the perseverance of the saints', writes Louise Berkhof, 'is to the effect that they whom God has regenerated and effectually called to a state of grace, can neither totally nor finally fall away from that state, but shall certainly persevere therein to the end and be eternally saved'.[1] Put negatively, Berkhof states, 'They whom have once been regenerated and effectually called by God to a state of grace can never completely fall from that state and thus fail to attain eternal salvation'.[2]

The Bible and the subordinate standards of the Christian church, which encapsulate the truth of the Bible, both teach the eternal security of all who are united to Christ in saving faith. The popular way of saying this is: 'Once saved, always saved'. In other words, true Christians can never lose their salvation. Why not? Because, as we have seen in our preceding chapters, salvation is a divine work, not a human one. It rests on what Christ has done—His finished work—and not on what we do.

Salvation is, as we have shown, a divine work from beginning to end, and Scripture teaches that the God who saves us is also the God who keeps us in the benefits of His salvation and will ensure that it is brought to its ultimate and eternal fruition. 'And I am sure that He who began a good work in you will bring it to completion at the day of Jesus Christ' (Philippians 1:6). God ensures that His people are saved and kept safe for time and eternity. Christians are described by Peter as those '... who by God's power are guarded through faith for a salvation ready to be revealed in the last time' (1 Peter 1:5). Jude fittingly concludes his short epistle by saying, 'Now to Him who is able to keep you from falling, and to present you without blemish before the presence of His glory with rejoicing' (Jude 24).

The fifth point of the five points of Calvinism—TULIP—is entitled 'The Perseverance of the Saints'. This point cannot be separated from the other points: our total inability to save ourselves; God's unconditional election, Christ's particular and definite atonement; and the Holy Spirit's irresistible calling. It teaches that the beneficiaries of God's saving grace will never fall out of the sphere of God's blessing but will persevere in the faith and reach glory at the last—this in spite of all the natural and supernatural opposition and barriers to their doing so. This *perseverance of the saints*, though begs the question: 'Why do believers persevere?' They are still only human. They are still plagued by indwelling sin, and the world, the flesh and the devil continually war against their spiritual welfare. However, believers persevere because God perseveres with them. Believers persevere because the preserving power of God persists in keeping them. Salvation is a matter of divine preservation. Jesus said, 'He who endures to the end will be saved' (Matthew 10:22), and true believers will indeed endure to the end, for God will enable them to do so by His continual working. A Christian's faith might be weak, but God's grip of grace on them is indomitable. His is a love that will not let us go. Every believer can relate to the Psalmist when he said, 'My soul clings to Thee; Thy right hand upholds me' (Psalm 63:8).

Whys and wherefores

The reality of the believer's eternal security stems from the very nature of the salvation God has bestowed on them. Eternal security is as much a matter of the logical implications of divine salvation as it is of the plain statements of Scripture. What do we mean? Well, consider the following. Romans 6:23 tells us that, 'The free gift of God is eternal life in Christ Jesus our Lord.' If we could fall away from this eternal life, it would not be *eternal* life. And if this eternal life is a gift of divine grace—a 'free gift'—it is unthinkable that God would give this gift to us one day and take it away from us on another. No, 'For the gifts and the call of God are irrevocable' (Romans 11:29).

Let us recap. The thesis of these pages is that salvation is divine, not human. As such, salvation can only be surer than sure, for '... it depends not upon man's will or exertion, but upon God's mercy' (Romans 9:16).

In chapter 3, we considered the doctrine of divine justification. Romans 8:33–34 affirms, 'Who shall bring any charge against God's elect? It is God who justifies; who is to condemn? ...' If a believer could indeed be lost, the insinuation is that Almighty God has changed His mind and reversed His declaration of 'not guilty' on us, invalidating the work of His Son. Such is unthinkable. Then, in chapter 4, we considered the doctrine of divine adoption: 'See what love the Father has given us, that we should be called children of God; and so we are' (1 John 3:1). If a believer could indeed be lost, the insinuation is that Almighty God takes us into His family one day and casts us out of it another. This is inconceivable! Believers are, because of Christ, both eternally 'not guilty' and eternally the children of God. Hence, Romans 8 ends with the triumphant affirmation that nothing either in this life or the next '... will be able to separate us from the love of God in Christ Jesus our Lord' (Romans 8:39). Romans 8:30 states that the believer's eternal welfare is so secure that they are as good as already in glory now! Under the guidance of the Holy Spirit, Paul puts our future glorification in the past tense! Romans 8:30 reads: 'And those whom He predestined He also called; and those whom He called He also justified; and those whom He justified He also glorified.' A.M. Toplady (1740–78) took up this glorious thought in his hymn 'A debtor to mercy alone'. The hymn is a hymn of Christian assurance:

My name from the palms of His hands
Eternity will not erase;
Impressed on His heart, it remains
In marks of indelible grace.
Yes! I to the end shall endure,
As sure as the earnest is given;
More happy, but not more secure
The glorified spirits in heaven.

Any objections?

Objections to the fact of the divine preservation of the believer sometimes run as follows:

'What about Mr So and So? He professed to be born again. He professed faith in Christ and was baptised and active in Christian service. Now though, he never attends church. If you asked him, he would say that it was just a phase he went through.'

The Lord Jesus actually anticipated those like Mr So and So. He would have us distinguish a profession of faith from the actual possession of faith. Professors fall away. Possessors continue. John, the apostle, spoke of those who '... went out from us, but they were not of us; for if they had been of us, they would have continued with us; but they went out, that it might be plain that they all are not of us' (1 John 2:19).

There is such a phenomenon as nominal Christianity— one who practises the externals of the faith but knows nothing of an inner *heart work* of God. Jesus said, 'Not every one who says to me, "Lord, Lord," shall enter the kingdom of heaven ...' (Matthew 7:21). Jesus also told His famous *Parable of the Sower*—how different people react to the word of the gospel. In this, some of the seed fell on rocky ground. What did Jesus mean? He explained: 'As for what was sown on rocky ground, this is he who hears the word and immediately receives it with joy; yet he has no root in himself, but endures for a while, and when tribulation or persecution arises on account of the word, immediately falls away' (Matthew 13: 20, 21). True conversion alone is a lasting conversion.

True faith: false faith

The Saviour thus anticipated a credible but false profession of faith. We think here of Demas. In Colossians 4:14, we see Demas as a companion of Paul, no doubt assisting him in Christian service. But sadly, some years later, in 2 Timothy 4:10, Paul writes, 'Demas, in love with this present world, has deserted me and gone to Thessalonica.' More happily however, the Saviour also anticipated a true profession of faith. He will build His church and this will be composed of those who truly belong to Him for time and eternity. These genuine Christians are described as Christ's sheep who know Him as their Good Shepherd. Jesus said of them: 'My sheep hear my voice, and I know them, and they follow me; and I give them eternal life, and *they shall never perish,* and no one shall snatch them out of my hand' (John 10:27, 28). The Greek here is most emphatic. Literally it says that Christ's sheep '... shall not never perish for ever'. It is the Holy Spirit's way of stressing that, if we belong to Jesus, we are eternally saved and eternally safe:

> Safe in Christ the weakest child
> Stands in all God's favour;
> All in Christ are reconciled
> Through that only Saviour.
>
> Safe in Christ! Safe in Christ!
> He's their glory ever;
> None can pluck them from His hand,
> They shall perish never.
>
> Henry D'Arcy Champney (1854–1942).

Saved forever!

If divine preservation was not a reality, we would be eternally lost, for, truth be told, we are incapable of keeping ourselves. Divine preservation is integral to divine salvation, for the God who saves us is also the God who keeps His own saved in the benefits of His salvation. Salvation in all its fullness is based on the goodwill of God, and God's will most surely will be done. Jesus said, 'This is the will of Him who sent me, that I should lose nothing of all that He has given me, but raise it up at the last day' (John 6:39). If salvation really is divine and not human, it is actually unthinkable that anyone saved by God's grace could ever lose their salvation, either in this life or the next. God in Christ saves. And God in Christ keeps, forever. With the Psalmist we may say, 'O give thanks to the LORD, for He is good, for His steadfast love endures for ever' (Psalm 136:1). With the apostle Paul we may say with confidence that, 'The Lord will rescue me from every evil and save me for His heavenly kingdom. To Him be the glory for ever and ever. Amen' (2 Timothy 4:18).

We shall give the last word on this subject to the *Westminster Confession of Faith*. Chapter 17 of this is entitled 'Of the Perseverance of the Saints'. It states:

> They, whom God hath accepted in His Beloved, effectually called and sanctified by His Spirit, can neither totally nor finally fall away from the state of grace; but shall certainly persevere therein to the end, and be eternally saved.
>
> This perseverance of the saints depends, not upon their own free will, but upon the immutability of the decree of election, flowing from the free and unchangeable love of God the Father; upon the efficacy of the merit and intercession of Jesus Christ; the abiding of the Spirit, and of the seed of God within them; and the nature of the covenant of grace; from all which ariseth also the certainty and infallibility thereof.[3]

Divine
benediction

For God so loved the world that He gave His only Son, that whoever believes in Him should not perish but have eternal life.

John 3:16

I came that they may have life, and have it abundantly.

John 10:10

The free gift of God is eternal life in Christ Jesus our Lord.

Romans 6:23

Eternal blessedness

'Eternal life' refers to a life of blessedness, both now and forever—and the Bible affirms that it is the Lord Jesus alone who is the key to knowing this blessedness. Jesus is the key to the art of living blessedly forever. Jesus is the key to a happy life, a happy death and a happy eternity.

Eternal life refers to salvation in all its fullness. It begins in this life, when we come to know and experience the salvation that Jesus came to bring, and it will be consummated in the age to come, in an age which we can only describe as *Paradise Restored*. As this eternal life is, '... the free gift of God ... in Christ Jesus our Lord' (Romans 6:23), it is indeed a divine benediction. It is a gift which this world can neither give to us nor take away from us. It is a gift from God Himself. It is a gift of the grace of God and the God of grace.

The greatest blessing

But what exactly is this *eternal life* which is the greatest blessing of all? The Greek for *eternal life* is *aionios zoe*. This refers not so much to a quantity of existence but a quality of existence, even though it is indeed unending. Eternal life refers to enjoying our true fulfilment of unblemished and unhindered fellowship with God our Maker. Being made in His image, eternal life refers to realising our chief end.

What is the chief end of man?

Man's chief end is to glorify God and to enjoy Him for ever' (Shorter Catechism).[1]

The Lion Concise Bible Encyclopaedia clarifies:

There is more to life than just physical existence. A relationship with God enables people to live life on a new level. This is the full, abundant life that Jesus came to bring. It is 'eternal life,' which Jesus offers as a free and permanent gift. Eternal life is life in a new dimension. 'God's life.' 'Whoever has the Son', says John, 'has this life.' It begins when a person becomes a Christian and survives death. It is an eternal relationship with God.[2]

Eternal life therefore is the difference between existing and really living life with a capital 'L.'

Fellowship with God

In a nutshell, eternal life refers to fellowship with God our

Maker—God, the fount of every blessing—both here and hereafter. Jesus said, 'This is eternal life, that they know Thee the only true God and Jesus Christ whom Thou hast sent' (John 17:3). According to the Bible, eternal life is both a present and a promised reality. It has facets to it which are both *realised* and *not yet*.

Eternal life is a present reality

John tells us that he wrote his Gospel with the express purpose '... that you may believe that Jesus is the Christ, the Son of God, and that believing you may have *life* in His name' (John 20:31). Then, later on, John tells us that he wrote his first epistle with the express purpose '... that you may know that you have eternal life' (1 John 5:13). In the first chapter of this epistle, we see that eternal life and fellowship with God are synonyms: 'We ... proclaim to you the eternal life ...' (1:2), '... so that you may have fellowship with us; and our fellowship is with the Father and with His Son Jesus Christ' (1:3). John's view that eternal life may be enjoyed here and now, ties in with the recorded words of His Master. For Jesus said, 'Truly, truly I say to you, he who hears my word and believes Him who sent Me, *has* eternal life; he does not come into judgment, but has passed from death to life' (John 5:24).

If eternal life refers to fellowship with God, we can see how it is inextricably linked with all the facets of salvation we have considered. To recap on some of these now:

- Divine remission: when our sins are forgiven, our fellowship with God is restored and we have peace with God.
- Divine imputation: free from the penalty of sin and clothed with Christ's righteousness, we have fellowship with God.
- Divine adoption: being brought into God's family, our earthly and eternal security is secure under His fatherly fellowship and care.
- Divine reconciliation: Jesus reconciles sinners— He brings us into eternal fellowship with God.
- Divine justification: Jesus puts us right with God, so that fellowship with God is established on a righteous basis.

Eternal life begins now, in our present experience. It begins at conversion. It begins when we put our faith in Jesus. Through Jesus and His saving work, we may enjoy fellowship with God with *not a cloud between*. 'But now in Christ Jesus you who once were far off have been brought near in the blood of Christ' (Ephesians 2:13).

> A mind at perfect peace with God,
> O what a word is this!
> A sinner reconciled through blood;
> This, this indeed is peace!
>
> By nature and by practice far,
> How very far from God;

Yet now by grace brought nigh to Him,
Through faith in Jesus' blood.

So near, so very near to God,
I cannot nearer be;
For in the person of His Son
I am as near as He.

So dear, so very dear to God,
More dear I cannot be;
The love wherewith He loves the Son;
Such is His love to me!

Why should I ever careful be,
Since such a God is mine?
He watches o'er me night and day,
And tells me "Mine is thine".'

Horatius Bonar (1808–89)

But the blessing of eternal life is not solely for now. So, finally, we will consider:Eternal life is a promised reality

The Christian Faith is forward looking. For the Christian the best is yet to be. The Christian's future is as bright as the promises of God! Truth be told, no Christian on earth is fully saved. We are saved in soul, but not in body. One day, though, we will be, for God has promised that we will be. The Bible holds out to us the prospect of living in a redeemed world and living in redeemed bodies. We will not always be fallen people living in a fallen world. Eden will yet be restored, 'because the creation itself will be set free from its bondage to decay and obtain the glorious liberty of the children of God' (Romans 8:21), 'and not only the creation, but we ourselves, who have the first fruits of the Spirit, groan inwardly as we wait for adoption as sons, the redemption of our bodies' (Romans 8:23). When will all this happen? At the end of this age when the Lord Jesus comes again in glory. 'We await a Saviour, the Lord Jesus Christ, who will change our lowly body to be like His glorious body, by the power which enables Him even to subject all things to Himself' (Philippians 3:20–21). What will this be like? It will be eternal life—fellowship with God unhindered, unhandicapped and unblemished by all that prevents our enjoyment of this—sin within and without—in this fallen world. No wonder that the prayer of Christians throughout the ages has always been 'Maranatha. Our Lord, come!' (1 Corinthians 16:22).

Eternal life therefore is both a present and a promised blessing—it is *the* divine benediction. It may be enjoyed now, but it will yet be enjoyed in a much fuller, richer way in the future, on a day firmly fixed in the divine plan of eternal redemption.

Eternal life refers to ultimate salvation. Eternal life refers to fellowship with God our Maker, and this is only possible in and through the Lord Jesus Christ, God's Son. 'There is salvation in no one else for there is no other name under heaven given among men by which we must be saved' (Acts 4:12).

Uncertain joys v solid joys

I write these words during an unprecedented time of recent history. My country, the United Kingdom, along with the rest of the world, is going through a pandemic—the Coronavirus, also known as Covid 19. This has seen much of what this world esteems being halted and curtailed. Social gatherings have been prohibited. Pubs, clubs and restaurants have been closed. Concerts have been cancelled. The esteemed football season has been scuppered. Many jobs have been lost and the economy has taken a downturn. Thousands of lives have been and are being lost ... We are currently under a *lockdown* to prevent the virus from spreading further. Normal living seems to be a distant memory. It goes to show the fragility, uncertainty and unreliability of all that this world esteems. But this is not the case with God's salvation—'... eternal life in Christ Jesus our Lord' (Romans 6:23). This is a gift which the world cannot give. And this is a gift which the world cannot take away. It is based on the finished work of Christ. It is the '... hope [that is, confident expectation based on the promises of God] of eternal life which God, who never lies, promised ages ago' (Titus 1:2). If our faith is in Christ, better and more glorious days await us. We will be raised to bliss and immortality—'made perfectly blessed in the full enjoying of God to all eternity' (*Shorter Catechism*).[3]

The last word will go to John Calvin, arguably the greatest theologian and expositor of the Bible ever:Our resurrection will be such that, raised from corruption into incorruptibility and from mortality into immortality, and being glorified both in our body and soul, the Lord will receive us into eternal blessedness, removed from all possibility of change and corruption.

We will have true and complete perfection of life, light and righteousness, seeing that we will be inseparably united to the Lord, who, like a spring that cannot run dry, contains within Himself all fullness.

This blessedness will be the kingdom of God, that kingdom which is filled with all light, joy, power and happiness. These realities are at the moment well beyond men's knowledge. We see them only as in a mirror and in a distorted manner until the day comes when the Lord will grant us to see His glory face to face.[4]

Soli Deo Gloria

Endnotes

Chapter 1

1 Westminster Divines, *Shorter Catechism*, 1648, (Banner of Truth edition, undated) Q.21

2 Westminster Divines, *Shorter Catechism*, 1648, (Banner of Truth edition, undated) Q.14

3 Westminster Divines, *Shorter Catechism*, Q.29

Chapter 2

1 Authors unknown, 'The Apostles Creed', *Book of Common Prayer*

2 John Calvin, *Truth for all Time*, 1537 (Edinburgh: Banner of Truth, Trans: Stuart Olyott, 1998) p.45

Chapter 3

1 Westminster Divines, *Shorter Catechism*, Q.33

2 Roderick Lawson, *Shorter Catechism with Scripture Proofs* (Belfast: Family Books Ltd, undated) p.25

3 Roland H. Bainton, *Here I Stand: A Life of Martin Luther*, (Nashville: Abingdon, 1950) p.49

Chapter 4

1 *Shorter Catechism*, Q.37

2 Roderick Lawson, *Shorter Catechism with Scripture Proofs*, p.26

3 Westminster Assembly, *Westminster Confession of Faith*, Chapter XII, (Glasgow: Free Presbyterian Publications, 1646) p.12

Chapter 5

1 William Ernest Henley, 'Invictus', Book of Verses, 1888, (https://poets.org/poem/invictus). Sourced: 04/08/21

2   Westminster Assembly, *Westminster Confession of Faith*, Chapter X,

3   Louis Berkhof, *Systematic Theology*, (Edinburgh: Banner of Truth, 1939) p.467

4   *Westminster Confession of Faith*, Chapter IX, paragraph III,

5   *Westminster Confession of Faith*, Chapter X,

Chapter 6

1   *Shorter Catechism*, Q.94

2   Roderick Lawson, *Shorter Catechism with Scripture Proofs*, p.55

3   *Martin Luther Quotes*, (https://citatis.com/a13178/069a60/). Sourced: 04/08/21

Chapter 7

1   T.C. Danson Smith, *Basic Fundamentals of the Faith*, (Edinburgh: B. Mcall Barbour, 1989) p.39

2   *Heidelberg Catechism*, Q. 10–11, 1563, (Protestant Reformed Churches of America, 1991 Edition)

Chapter 10

1   *Westminster Confession of Faith*, Chapter X,

2   *Shorter Catechism*, Q.89

Chapter 11

1   Louis Berkhof, *Systematic Theology*, p.545

2   Louis Berkhof, *Systematic Theology*, p.546

3   Westminster Assembly, 'Of the Perseverance of the Saints', *Westminster Confession of Faith*, Chapter XVII,

Chapter 12

1   *Shorter Catechism*, Q.1

2   Pat Alexander (ed.), *The Lion Encyclopaedia of the Bible*, (Tring: Lion Publication, 1978), p.151

3   *Shorter Catechism*, Q.38

4   John Calvin, *Truth for all Time*, p.47